The Church Book

By Dr. O. D. Woods

ISBN
Hardcover: 978-1-965560-23-5
Paperback: 978-1-965560-24-2

PAGE LEFT BLANK INTENTIONALLY

Contents

Introduction

This book's purpose is to guide the church and leaders to a thorough understanding of the Church's work, its rules, and regulations, regardless of any denomination. It can be helpful to any group of people in any congregation.

After being closely affiliated with Church work, as a pastor for nearly fifty years, and as a moderator of a district association for twenty-five years, I want to share some of my valuable experiences with you.

I was born and raised in the small country town of Harris, Oklahoma, with a population of approximately 300 people. I was raised in the Antioch Baptist Church and attended the Church of God in Christ there from the age of approximately seven years old. I joined the church at the age of eight. Under a shade tree on Sunday evenings, a group of us children have our own version of church, and I was selected as their pastor by the young group.

I was called into the Ministry in 1975 and became a pastor a year later in 1976. There is a vast difference between being a preacher and a pastor! While a pastor's role incredibly varies, a preacher is one who preaches. Simply put, all pastors are preachers, but not all preachers are pastors. Preachers technically are the ones who proclaim and spread the Word of God. The term pastor is rooted in its meaning or origin as a shepherd. Since "shepherd" is associated with an overseer of the flock, it is appropriate that an overseer of a congregation is called a shepherd. Pastors, being shepherds, guide their church members toward salvation. Technically, they function as the physical, spiritual, relations, and social administrator of a congregation. They are the local church leaders, and they should be qualified to give counsel to those in need of spiritual, emotional, and even, in some cases, their mental and physical well-being. Therefore, the pastor is a person with a gift for taking care of people, primarily with respect to their Spiritual lives, but also gives comfort, guidance, and wisdom in day-to-day life. At the same time, the preacher is someone who devotes time simply proclaiming the Word of God. Once again, all pastors are preachers, but not all preachers are pastors.

Being called to pastor opened many avenues for me to be skillful in my task as a pastor. Many frequently asked questions by church people never receive settled answers. I want to discuss some of these questions and answers, for which I have thoroughly researched studies and experiences.

First, let us look at Chapter 1, which deals with Church Finances.

Chapter 1: Church Finances

Questions and Answers

I. Question- Who can decide to sell the church if the Church disbands or under other circumstances? How can the proceeds be divided?

   A. In the first place, I asked this question to help us understand who owns the church. This process of ownership is Christ. The Lord is the owner; therefore, selling the building or any church property should be handled by the guidance of the Spirit of God. Although the registered agent can act on behalf of the church, the remaining members must ensure that this person does only what is directed by the body.

II. Question- Who are the authorized signers of the church bank account?

   A. Again, the remaining members must ensure that the signers do only what has been voted on by the body.

III. Question- Should the Deacon Staff maintain control of the finances of the church when a trustee board is created?

   A. The answer to this question is that most Baptist churches are Membership Corporations. This means that the membership determines who handles the church's corporate responsibilities. If, through their by-laws, the membership places this responsibility in the hands of the deacons, the trustees have no oversight in that area.

IV. Question- Should the pastor sign checks?

A. This matter is both personal will and available personnel. Is the church so small that there are not enough competent people to fill the position? If this is the case, then the pastor must do whatever is necessary to take care of the business decently and in order. However, the best approach for the pastor is to oversee the finance department rather than directly manage it. They should have oversight but not be directly involved. Ideally, the pastor should not be a signer on financial accounts but should still be aware of every check that is issued.

V. Question- Should the Financial giving of church members be made known to the entire church?

A. Sometimes, in an effort to provide financial transparency, individuals giving may be made public. There is nothing legally improper with this practice. However, this practice may not be appropriate for some. Therefore, any member who wishes not to have their financial information made public should simply make that known to the pastor and/or finance department. That request should be immediately honored.

VI. Question- If the church service close down for one or more Sundays, and the church pays the pastor's salary for those missed Sundays, is the church required to pay the musician(s) as well?

A. First of all, no one in the church should be compared to the pastor's position. He is the under shepherd and should be the only one treated as such, whether financially or otherwise.

Chapter 2: Church Procedures

Questions and Answers

Let's just jump right in and look at these important and frequently asked questions.

I. Question- Can a church meeting be called without the pastor's consent?

A. No. A church meeting called without the Pastor's consent must be done by the Church Clerk by the order of the majority vote of Deacons, having obtained a sufficient number of signatures from the membership to reach a quorum.

II. Question-What is the procedure for terminating the pastor?

A. It is generally accepted that the Deacon Board can call a church meeting to present a petition for termination and ask for a vote. If the Deacon Board won't call a meeting, the Church Clerk can. Two-thirds of the church membership must approve a petition circulated by the clerk to set the meeting date. After the notice is sent, the date must be at least two weeks later.

III. Question- What positions in the Baptist church can the Minister appoint without church members' input or vote?

A. The only biblical office is that of the deacon. Every church should determine the scope of appointments vs. elections. Auxiliaries or groups whose ministry is group-specific may be appointed or recommended to the church by that group (e.g., the choir president). Leaders of groups or ministries that have a broader impact on the entire ministry of the church should be elected by the church. For example, Mission ministry. The church should ratify all appointments and elections. That way, the church maintains responsibility for all of its leadership.

Chapter 3: Church Administration

Questions and Answers

Business usually involves money. There have been many issues in the church that involve paid staff. Let's look at some of the questions and answers on this subject.

I. Question—To whom should paid staff report in the church? I am trying to understand the scripture in the Book of Acts, which says, "Look among you and find seven men of good report whom we may appoint over this business."

A. The word "business" in the 6th chapter of Acts refers to the meeting of the needs of the Hellenistic Christians who were murmuring. It more universally refers to the responsibility of those selected to serve the body, freeing the Pastors to prayer and the Word. When it comes to reporting of staff through a chain of command, it really depends upon whether they are considered to be "pastoral" staff, maintenance staff, office staff, etc. Generally, all staff report to the Pastor through the particular ministry leader except for Pastoral staff, who report directly to the Pastor. For example, The building engineer would report to the Chairman of Trustees, who may have oversight of the building. That Chairman will, of course, consult with and report directly to the Pastor because he will have direct responsibility over Worship and Church administration.

Church Planting

II. Question-How do you start a new church?

A. The New Hiscox Guide for Baptist Churches (Judson Press) outlines these steps for starting a new church:

1. Meet regularly for worship, reflection, and prayer. Test your purpose, seek counsel, and seek spiritual guidance.

2. Establish a responsible committee to develop official documents, such as constitutions, covenants, by-laws and articles of procedure. This group will also take care of the articles of incorporation (if needed), tax-exempt status, etc.

3. The constituting or charter members of the church should transfer their membership by letter from their previous church to the new church.

4. An official constituting meeting should be announced and publicized and should include a full worship service preceding the business. A vote should be held to constitute the new church properly, and the documents developed should be brought forward for approval. Following this, officers of the church should be elected. If there is no pastor yet, a committee should be elected to recommend pastoral leadership. Conclude the meeting with a hymn and a prayer.

5. The church's leadership should stick to the bylaws and constitution created, communicate with the congregation about what is going on, and seek prayerful support.

6. Petition the denomination you want to affiliate with for membership.

7. Continue to diligently establish goals, programs, procedures, and effective review processes.

Chapter 4: Pastor and Other Clergy:

Questions and Answers

In my almost fifty years of preaching, I have heard preachers called everything from Reverend to Bishop, Dr, or Pastor. Does the title fit the task? Or is it appropriate to address your pastor or a preacher by his first name? The answer is "NO". Out of respect for the office, the Preacher should be respected. If he is not respected in public, he is called by his first name. Let's look at these questions and answers along with others that come with the position of Pastor.

Types of Clergy

I. Question- What is the difference between pastors and bishops in the Baptist tradition?

A. In the Baptist tradition, pastors and bishops are, for all intents and purposes, the same. In many non-Baptist denominations, i.e., Methodists, Episcopalians, Catholics, etc., a bishop appoints pastors to churches in a designated region and governs over them. Episcopacy is the governance of churches by bishops (consistent with the faith traditions of Episcopalians, Methodists, etc.). Episcopacy is not consistent with the beliefs of National Baptists, where each church/congregation is responsible for governing itself.

II. Question- What is the difference between an Associate Minister and an Assistant Pastor? Do they have defined or generally accepted roles? What scripture or resource supports this?

A. There is no scriptural reference for either Assistant Pastor or Associate Minister. Biblically, there is only one Pastor. He may appoint other ministers to responsible offices for the purpose of carrying out the work and ministry of the Church, as Paul did with those who traveled with him. The term "Assistant Pastor" is generally used incorrectly. The Assistant Pastor is usually one on paid staff, selected by the Pastor and accepted or voted by the Church to such office. What we usually mean when we say being appointed to more pastoral responsibility than other associate ministers. By the way, an associate minister is any minister who is a member of the Church.

III. Question- Are licensed ministers considered "clergy"?

A. In the strict sense, "clergy" are ordained Christian ministers. However, in practice, we consider those who have been separated from the laity to be clergy. The license to preach is always under the control and auspices of the granting local Church. As such, its expiration, lack thereof, or recall of the same is completely at the discretion of that local body. There is no expiration or recall of the ordained Baptist minister. This is why ordination should not be granted lightly or haphazardly.

IV. Question- What is the role of a Pastor Emeritus?

A. There are no "rules" or guidelines specific to emeritus pastors except what the church determines the roles and responsibilities. However, the term "emeritus" generally carries with it a reduction in responsibility and income associated with the position. Here's a definition of emeritus for you from Wikipedia, the online dictionary (http://en.wikipedia.org/wiki/Emeritus): Emeritus is a title given to a retired professor, bishop, or other professional. Emerita was used for women but is rarely used nowadays. The term is used when a person of importance in a given profession retires so that his or her former rank is still in his or her title. Generally, the term emeritus also signifies a reduction in work responsibilities and income.

Minister License, Covering, and Ordination

I had the opportunity to ordain a minister this year who came from a non-denominational church. A Baptist church selected him as their pastor. Because I am the Moderator of our district, the church came to me for advice and guidance. My suggestion was to license the minister, ordain him, and then later install him as their pastor. The following material will be helpful in guiding pastors in the steps to licensing and ordaining a minister.

V. Question- Can someone with a minister's license obtain from the Internet pastor a Baptist Church?

A. No one is licensed to PASTOR a Baptist Church. A license is granted to an individual by the church or denominational organization to which that person belongs, having given "evidence" of a call to ministry. After proof of effective ministry has been, either through faithful service and/or education, one may be set aside for ordination. A council convened by the church may do ordination or may be conferred by the Pastor/Church. Pastors are selected from those who have been ordained. An online license is usually a sign that the individual was either not a part of a church or the church was unwilling to recognize their calling. Any church considering a person who was licensed online for the position should be very wary and investigate the ministerial experience of the candidate.

VI. Question- Can a Minister's license be revoked? If so, on what grounds can this request be made, and what process should take place?

A. When granted a preaching license, it's given by a church for the individual to prove their calling. The license ALWAYS belongs to the Church until that person undergoes ordination into the Gospel Ministry. Consequently, a Baptist Church may revoke the license to preach. There are several grounds on which a license may be recalled. A few examples are unscriptural conduct, failure to adhere to the tenets and principles of the Baptist faith, or incompetence. The Baptist church is charged to scrutinize a licentiate very carefully because once that individual is ordained; there is no adjudicatory that can revoke ordination.

VII. Question- Should a licensed minister be called "Reverend" before he/she has been ordained?

A. You may call them anything you desire. Is it appropriate? No.

VIII. Question- What support does the Convention offer for new female ministers?

A. The Convention does not offer specific support for female ministers at this time. However, there are many learning opportunities available for you through the National Baptist Congress of Christian Education Annual Session and your state and District Congress meetings. Check out the Young Ministers Division and Minister's Division at the Congress Session. In the meantime, you may find this online resource helpful to you: Gifted for Leadership, an online resource especially for women in the ministry.

Ordination

IX. Question- What is the difference between "licensed" and "ordained" ministers?

A. Licensed ministers are permitted to "practice" their calling under the authority of a local Pastor. As such, they are not permitted to do communion, baptize, or commit bodies unless given authority to do so by their local Pastor. They are not legally allowed to perform marriages. The Church issues the license, and it can be recalled by the Church. Once a minister is ordained, he/she may legally perform marriages and can take charge of all Church functions and ordinances without the approval of another minister. The ordination belongs to the minister, and any other Baptist body cannot reclaim such. This is why it is so important to carefully examine all licentiates before they are ordained. You can correct mistakes when a minister is licensed. It becomes difficult, if not impossible, to do so after they are ordained.

VII. Question- When Does a Licensed minister need to be ordained?

A. A Licentiate is generally recommended for ordination because any one of the following reasons is valid:

1. The licentiate receives a call to pastor a Church.

2. The licentiate graduated from the Seminary and is assigned or employed in an area requiring ordination.

3. The pastor of the Church where the licentiate serves has a need for additional aid in areas requiring ordination.

NOTE: Because no administrative body can de-frock an ordained Baptist preacher, Baptist churches are encouraged to be deliberate and cautious in the ordination process.

VIII. Question- Should a minister be set aside first before being ordained? How long should he be set aside?

A. "Within the Baptist tradition, when an individual expresses a "call" to the ministry, they are granted a "trial" or initial sermon at the will of the church. Based upon the outcome of that sermon, the Church may grant that individual a license to preach. This license affords the person the privilege to exercise and make full proof of their call to ministry. Licensure is "owned" by the church and can be granted or revoked by the church on behalf of an individual. A licensed minister may be ordained when they have, either through education or service, enrolled to the level sufficient to satisfy the church, and there is a need in the church for an ordained minister. This recognition that the individual is an authentic minister of the gospel. Essentially, a licentiate is on a trial period. They are not official ministers until ordination. Unlike licensure, ordination is "owned" by the minister, not the church. The church grants one ordination and cannot take it away. "If by set aside" you are referring to a waiting period between licensing and ordination, the answer is "yes," until "they have either through education or matriculated to the level sufficient to satisfy the church and there is a need in the church for an ordained minister."

IX. Question- Does a minister have to be ordained to become a pastor?

    A. If a licensed minister is called to pastor, he should be ordained before assuming responsibility. An unordained minister cannot carry out the pastor's responsibilities.

X. Question- Can people who are not ordained ministers conduct the ordinance of baptism?

    A. "Only Ordained Deacons or Licensed Ministers under the authority of an Ordained Pastor/Minister may conduct the ordinance of Baptism. "If the Ordained Pastor/Minister is present and leading the baptismal service (actually says those words), the physical immersion may be done by anyone. In fact, Jesus Himself never baptized anyone. He let His disciples do it for Him."

XI. Question- What happens to a licensed pastor who wasn't ordained before the death or retirement of the pastor?

    A. In the event of the death of the Pastor, the minister in charge or the chair of deacons carries out the administrative duties. If the church was planning to ordain the preacher, the chairman may organize a council of ordained ministers for that purpose. It is recommended that the church ask its district moderator to convene for that purpose. It is recommended that the church ask its district moderator to convene the council. If there were no formal plans to ordain prior to the pastor's death and no pressing need for the church, the ordination should be put on hold until a new pastor is selected and let that person handle it. In the event that the pastor retired before ordaining the licentiate, the pastor should have left instructions for the ordination of licensed preachers. If he did not, there must be some reason why. The officers in charge should seek his input and then, if they are going to move forward, proceed as previously outlined.

XII. Question- Can a National Baptist church select a pastor who is not Ordained or Licensed by the National Baptist Church but has been ordained and licensed by another denomination?

A. A Baptist Church may call a preacher as Pastor and ask his current Church to ordain him prior to his assuming the pastorate. However, only a Baptist organization can ordain a minister to the Baptist faith. No Baptist Church should call a minister from another denomination unless they are willing to ordain him themselves and if he/she is willing to accept Baptist doctrine, principle, and polity.

XIII. Question- Can a National Baptist minister be covered by a minister from a different denomination?

A. "Covering" is in reference to the male representative head covering in the Bible. Adam was Eve's "covering." Consequently, God held Adam responsible for Eve eating the fruit. Biblically, husbands are the "covering" for wives. In the Baptist Church, one can rise no higher than an ordained Pastor. As such, the only covering is that of the local church. A minister from another Baptist denomination (e.g., Southern Baptist, Progressive, etc.) can be considered as Pastoring a National Baptist

Church as long as he/she is an ordained Baptist minister.

XIV. Question- What are the qualifications for ordained ministers?

A. The Convention doesn't have a policy on the qualifications for ordained ministers. This determination is left up to the individual churches to decide. However, an often cited and used resource among Convention churches is the Hiscox Guide. There is an extensive section in this book on the qualifications of ministers and the ordination process that suggests that requiring a minimum amount of education is not only reasonable but required to qualify the minister for service. "Intellectual capability may not be the first qualification for the ministry. But the ministry demands the best of the mind and skill of those who exercise it. Academic preparation appropriate to the demands of the work and the expectations of the community is necessary. The specific requirements may be different from church to church and from denomination to denomination. But all ministers should be willing to meet and desire to exceed such preparation for the effectiveness of their ministry. Ministry should be built on academic preparation and continuing commitment to education throughout a ministry…" (Goodwin. 1995. The New Hiscox Guide for Baptist Churches, pp.56-57).

XV. Question- Can a minister hold an ordination in more than one denomination simultaneously? Does a National Baptist Ordained Minister lose his ordination if he subsequently is ordained by another denomination?

A. A Baptist ordained minister does not necessarily lose his/her original ordination once leaving his denomination to join a different denomination. However, since each Baptist church is autonomous, whether a Baptist pastor from his original denomination chooses to accept his or her credentials upon returning to the original denomination in which he was ordained is up to that pastor. He or she can maintain an original ordination, as well as, secure an ordination from a different denomination at the same time based on acceptance by both denominations. Today's ordination credentialing is far more liberal than it used to be due to new denominations, non-denominations, and Spiritual Centers.

Baptist Ordination Council Overview

In Baptist churches, according to the Baptist Faith and Message by Hershel H. Hobbs, "The officers in a local New Testament church are pastors and deacons (Philippians 1:1). The same office is variously called bishop, elder, or pastor."1. These two officers are generally placed in their respective offices by the local congregation through a service of ordination. The model for this service is found in Acts 6:1-7. The term ordination is the setting aside of an individual for a particular purpose. The purpose of ordination for an individual is to signify a sense of calling by God and to commit their life to a particular ministry. For the local congregation, it is the acknowledgment, approval, and authorization for the individual to serve the church in ministry. In the New Testament, there is no prescribed procedure for the service of ordination other than what is depicted in Acts 6. It was something the congregation was called upon to do rather than an appointment by an individual or group. The church was charged with selecting men whose walk with the Lord was respected, wise and demonstrated by lifestyle that they were full of the Holy Spirit. The one particular thing that stands out ceremonially is the laying on of hands. This was frequently used in the New Testament as a public and formal act of setting aside for ministry individuals (Acts 6:6, 13:3, 1 Timothy 4:14 and 5:22, and 2 Timothy 1:6). Ordination is (1) a function of the local church, (2) It is an open and public service, (3) Consists of the laying on of hands, and (4) It is for deacons and ministers of the gospel. Traditionally, the ordination service consists of two parts: the coming together of the ordaining council and the Ordination service. This is true for the ordination of deacons and ministers. The difference between the two services is whether the local congregation chooses to make the deacon ordination service local or invite others to participate. Another difference is that there may be multiple individuals ordained in a deacon ordination, as opposed to only one in a ministry ordination.

The Minister's Ordaining Council:

The ordaining council should be composed of ministers and deacons from various churches that convene for the explicit purpose of ordaining a person to the gospel ministry. This council shall convene before the actual ordination service. During the organization of the Ordaining Council, the first order of business should be the election of officers. Officers for the Ordaining The council shall be the moderator, who will preside over the council and the service. A questioner to examine the candidate. And a secretary/clerk to record the actions of the Council.

Questioning the Candidate:

The moderator will ask the candidate to present himself before the council either by sitting in front of the council or by standing behind the pulpit before the congregation. This will be determined by either a public or private examination. The candidate should be able to use biblical texts to support his position on any theological question as requested. Sample questions include:

1. Tell of your conversion experience and your call to the ministry

2. What do you believe about the Bible?

3. What is unique about Jesus Christ?

4. Who is the Holy Spirit, and how does He operate in the life of a believer?

5. What is a New Testament Church, and what is its mission?

6. What are the ordinances of the church? And what is their significance?

7. Share how and when you shared Christ with someone.

8. What do you believe about sin and its effects on humanity?

9. Tell of your involvement in Christian ministry through the local church?

10. What is your belief about and the practice of Christian Stewardship?

11. What do you believe about Heaven?

12. What do you believe about Hell?

13. What do you believe about the second coming of Christ?

14. How do you personally practice the spiritual disciplines of prayer, fasting, and bible study?

15. How would you handle criticism and conflict in your ministry?

16. How is a Baptist church different than a Catholic or a non-denominational church?

17. How do your wife and family feel about your calling to the ministry?

The floor is then open for questions from members of the Ordaining Council. The candidate is then dismissed while the council formulates its recommendation. The action is recorded by the secretary/clerk, and each member of the ordaining council signs the certificate.

It is entirely up to the ordination council which questions to present for the questioning period. The following sample Q&A with Explanation format and content serves well and is suitable for both the council and the candidate, provided that the candidate for Baptist ordination wholeheartedly agrees with the stated answers provided.

Baptist Ordination Questions and Answers

Question no. 1) How many ordinances are observed in the modern Baptist Church?

Answer:

There are two ordinances: Baptism and the Lord's Supper.

Question no. 2) Do you believe in baptism by sprinkling or by immersion?

Answer:

By Immersion

Question no. 3) Define Baptism.

Answer:

The meaning of the word Baptism in the Greek language means essentially to dip or immerse, not sprinkle.

Explanation- The New Testament suggests that people went down into the water to be immersed rather than have water brought to them to be poured or sprinkled.

Question no. 4) What Avenue leads to Salvation?

Answer:

The life of Jesus and the belief in his body and blood offered on the Cross are the only ways to Salvation.

Question no. 5) What does an ordained minister do?

Answer:

An ordained minister performs church rites and religious sacraments. The responsibilities include performing baptism, acting as an officiant in weddings and funerals- Engage the congregation in the practice of their faith by giving sermons and teaching.

Question no. 6) What is a New Testament Church?

Answer:

A New Testament Church is a church that is structured and governed in accordance with New Testament principles and doctrines.

Question no. 7) What does the Spirit of God mean to you?

Answer:

The Holy Spirit works in us by peeling away our sinful characteristics and replacing them with Godly ones. His work in us makes us more like Jesus. The Holy Spirit gives us the power to witness. Just as Acts 1:8 mentions, the Holy Spirit empowers Christians to be effective witnesses for Christ.

Question no. 8) What is the Baptist endeavor?

Answer:

The Baptist endeavor is based on the belief, practice, emphasis, and organization of the teaching of the Bible.

Explanation- Baptists desire to be as close to the New Testament model for an individual Christian and for a church that is humanly possible with God's help through the instruction and empowerment of the Holy Spirit.

Question no. 9) What is the meaning of autonomous?

Answer:

The word autonomous comes from two Greek words that mean "self" and "law". It means self-governing or self-directing.

Explanation—An autonomous church is not absolutely autonomous because it should always recognize Jesus's control and authority as Lord.

Question no. 10) What is the benefit of Baptist autonomy?

Answer:

Autonomy allows each congregation to determine how best to reach and minister to the community in which it exists. Church autonomy reinforces the fact that in a Baptist Church, each member is responsible for the Church, especially the Pastor.

Chapter 5: Church Leaders and Staff

Questions and Answers

There are many guides and manuals that can help church leaders find helpful information concerning the positions and auxiliaries in the modern church. I have listed some of which this book should be included. Let us also look at some of the frequently asked questions pertaining to these positions and auxiliaries in the church.

I. Question- Where can I get Information about the role of Church Leaders, including Trustees, Deacons, Ushers, Treasurers, Secretaries, etc.?

A. *The Hiscox Guide for Baptist Churches* will have some resources. Also, "The Busy Pastors Guide" printed by the Sunday School Publishing Board will be helpful (of course, the BIBLE is an assumed resource). You may contact the SSPB directly concerning your specific book request and those mentioned above:

1. *Church Structure, Management, Constitution and By-Laws Resources*

   Goodwin, Everett C.1995

2. *The New Hiscox Guide for Baptist Churches*

   Valley Forge, PA: Judson Press Goodwin, Everett C. 1995

3. *The Baptist Church Directory: A Guide to the Doctrines and Discipline, Officers and Ordinances, Principles and Practices of Baptist Churches*

Ann Arbor: University of Michigan Press Hiscox, Edward T. 1981

4. ***The Hiscox Guide for Baptist Churches*** Valley Forge, PA: Judson Press

5. ***Baptist Beliefs***

    Mullins, E. Y. 1983 Valley Forge, PA: Judson Press

6. ***A New Baptist Church Manual***

    Valley 1986 Forge, PA: Judson Press

7. ***The Baptist Standard Church Directory and Busy Pastor's Guide***

    A. M. Townsend [and] E. W. D. Isaac Nashville Sunday School Publishing Board

Deacons

I. Question- Where can I find information on the process for ordaining a Deacon?

A. There is a book called ***The Baptist Deacon*** written by Robert E. Naylor and published by Broadman Press of Nashville, TN. For more information on selection and ordination, pay close attention to Chapter Three. You may also consult ***Church Officers At Work*** by Glenn H. Asquith published by Judson Press. Additional information can be found in these often-used resources:

1. ***The New Hiscox Guide for Baptist Churches*** Valley Forge, PA: Judson Press Goodwin, Everett C. 1995

2. ***The Baptist Church Directory: A Guide to the Doctrines and Discipline, Officers and***

Ordinances, Principles and Practices of Baptist Churches Ann Arbor: University of Michigan Press Hiscox, Edward T. 1981

I. Question- Can a divorced person be a deacon in the church?

A. The answer to this question, like so many other questions in the autonomous tradition of Baptist Church doctrine, will be based on the local church's theological understanding and tradition. Its theological understanding and tradition are usually driven by past and present Pastors' theology regarding the Office of Deacon.

Conservative interpretations of First Timothy 3:12, from which this question arises, take these words literally. (This surprises me since these interpreters do not take into consideration the larger context, verses 8-12. If they did, I doubt that we would have any deacons that actually qualify for the office.) My personal belief, as informed by Church historians and theologians who have studied cultural context as an important interpretation tool, is:

1. This rule does not make it necessary that a deacon even has to have a wife to serve as a Deacon, nor
2. Imply that he cannot continue his office once re-married, either after the death of the first wife or after a legal, scriptural divorce of the first wife.

Peter is possibly establishing the rule that he (both pastor and deacon) should have "one legal wife at a time," along with a particular set of Christian family values. This would be a way of excluding certain "wanna-be (s)" from becoming elders, pastors, deacons, etc., of churches:

1. Who planned on becoming "polygamists"

2. Who were present polygamists, or
3. Who had divorced their wives for reasons other than scriptural law allowed and married others.

Polygamy and divorce in the first century were quite common among Jews and non-Jews due to Greek culture. In spite of what the Jewish law commanded Leviticus 21:13-14, Jews (and non-Jews, for that matter) were not easily convinced that their right to marry more than one woman at a time should be given up in order to become a Christian. And though polygamy and divorces were not lawful per Jewish scripture, they became especially scandalous in officers of the early century churches.

This was the situation that had to be corrected if the church was to grow. It is the above background that helps us understand that in the early formation of the church as a distinct religious institution from the Jewish Temple faith, Christian officers like the Apostle Paul were laying rules and laws. They made it quite clear that Jewish and non-Jewish marriage liberalism would not infect Christian office-holding. Christian officers of faith would be held to certain standards, one of which would be, "no polygamy allowed" and no key office holding by those who refuse to give up their other culturally defined values and ways.

For this and some more complicated theological reasons, one interpretation of 1 Timothy 3:12 would be that a divorced deacon was not prohibited from serving the Office of Deacon if his divorce was on acceptable Christian grounds as understood through scripture. Such a person would also not be prohibited from remarrying if he remarried a Christian woman and committed as a Deacon to being governed by the rest of the values stated in 1 Timothy 3:8-12 (to the best of his knowledge and ability, I might add). Again, the above is one interpretation that many Baptist churches go by.

II. Question- Can the deacons call a meeting without informing the Pastor?

A. The Deacons are the Pastor's helpers and as such, gain their authority from the Pastor's office. Since they get their "marching orders" from the Pastor, they have nothing to talk about without either the pastor's presence or knowledge. Actually, only two persons may call a Deacons' meeting: The Pastor or the Chairman of Deacons. The chairman should not do so without the Pastor's knowledge. Part of the Deacon's responsibility is to promote harmony within the Church. The calling of a private meeting without the Pastor's knowledge not only fails to promote harmony but, in fact, disrupts the harmony. Even if the meeting were totally innocent, it can have a significant negative effect on the Congregation. Member will surmise that either the Deacons are up to something or that the Pastor is up to something. Either way, disunity ensues. That is why it is so vitally important for the Deacons and the Pastor to have open communication. Consequently, any deviation from that process should be dealt with swiftly and emphatically.

III. Question- Can a deacon extend the invitation to discipleship after the sermon is preached and ordained ministers are present?

A. Deacons can extend the invitation to discipleship or membership in any Baptist church. However, if an ordained minister is present, they should defer to them.

Deaconess

IV. Question- What is the role of the Deaconess in the church?

A. There is a general consensus regarding the Black Baptist Church's understanding of the character of the Deaconess if, for no other reason, the character of a Deaconess is spelled out very clearly in I Timothy 3:11.

1. In this passage, the word women is interpreted by Baptists to mean "wives" of male deacons.

2. Traditionally, the Deaconess is the female wife of her husband, who is a Deacon. Traditionally, she assists in the following areas:
   a. Assists her husband in home and hospital visits
   b. Assists the Deacons in carrying out Baptism and the Lord's Supper.
   c. Provide spiritual counseling to females of the church
   d. Provide instruction for single women, wives, and young teens in church etiquette, church protocol, and general matters of faith.

1. In the last 20 years or so, there has been a growing defection from the traditional understanding of the Deaconess and, therefore, the role of the Deaconess. This departure stems from a re-visitation of the texts that have been traditionally interpreted as deaconess or servant when the Bible passage is referring to women.

For example, Romans 16:1 states, according to the King James Version, "I commend unto you Phoebe our sister, which is a servant of the church which is in

Cenchreae..." Some Baptists interpret servant to mean deaconess because the word in Greek, diakonos, is the same word used in other places for a male Deacon. Such is the case in I Timothy 3:8. Since some pastors' theology of ministry leadership, especially ordained leadership, does not permit women to be ordained, Phoebe could not be called a Deacon, so they have given female servants the name deaconess. This decision to give female servants the name deaconess to distinguish them from male deacons who are ordained they justified theologically by additional New Testament texts; Jesus' own decision to not call women to his side as his special appointed/ordained disciples, and Black Baptist church tradition. Pastors who have decided not to make a gender distinction between males and females have justified ordaining female deacons on the basis of theological interpretations of texts, as well as precedents established by the theological interpretation of the early church fathers. For example, the early church Father, John Chrysostom, in Homilies on Romans 31 (on Rom 16:1; late 4th century), understood diakonos to be a term of rank and that "even women are instituted deacons in the church." Ignatius, Bishop of Rome at the turn of the century, twice refers to a deacon of one church serving as an ambassador to another church. (Ignatius Letter to the Philadelphians 10:1; Letter to the Ephesians 2.1) Women were also among the ranks of deacons in the Ephesians church: "Women (deacons), likewise, are to be worthy of respect, not slanderers, temperate, and trustworthy in everything" (I Timothy 3:11 my translation.). Dr. Linda Belville, in her article, Women Leaders in the Bible, DISCOVERING

BIBLICAL EQUALITY: COMPLEMENTARITY WITHOUT HIERARCHY, INTERVARSITY PRESS 2004, P.122) states, "That Paul is speaking of women in a recognized leadership role is apparent not only from the listing of credentials but also from the fact that these credentials are duplicates of those listed for male deacons in I Timothy 3:8-10. Also, the Greek word order of I Timothy 3:8 and 11 is identical: "[Male] deacons likewise [diakonous hosautos] must be serious, not double-tongued, not indulging in much wine...Women likewise must be serious, not slanders, but temperate" (I Tim 3:8,11 NRSV). Clement of Alexandria (second-third century) says, "For we know what the honorable Paul in one of his letters to Timothy prescribed regarding women deacons." Clement of Alexandria Strategies 3.6.53).

V. Question- Does a Deaconess have to be married to a Deacon in the church in order to serve?

A. The role of Deaconess varies from Church to Church depending on the local polity. In general, a Deaconess is a woman, selected by the Church, who performs the functions of a male Deacon in instances where it would be inappropriate for a male to do so (dressing female candidates for baptism). As such, there is no requirement for the woman's husband to be a Deacon member of the local Church. Some Churches, however, fill the office of Deaconess solely on the basis of being married to a Deacon. In such cases, the Church determines if it requires marriage to a Deacon of its local congregation or any Deacon anywhere. Finally, some Churches do not use Deaconesses at all, opting to let the Mother's Board fulfill this function.

Mother of The Church

VI. Question- What are the role and qualifications of the Mother of the church?

A. This is an honorary position in the church. The qualifications and responsibilities will vary based on the church's interpretation and ministry needs.

1. This position can be a lifetime once the person is either elected by the church membership or appointed by the pastor. If elected, the church may reaffirm the appointments during the annual church meeting.
2. There may be multiple Mothers in the church.
3. The criterion for appointment or election is established by the church in keeping with sound Christian doctrine and varies by church. Mothers are often widows or older unmarried women, but this is not necessarily a requirement.
4. Often, a Mother's Club or Ministry is formed that may do any or all the following things:
   a. Assist in the nurturing of members, especially young teens and youth.
   b. Engage in special ministry projects of a missionary nature.
   c. Visit the sick d. Assist in the kitchen during the time of funerals, as well as carry flowers from the sanctuary to the funeral cars
   d. Prepare Thanksgiving and/or Christmas meals for the home-bound or at the church
   e. Engage in whatever duties are assigned and deemed appropriate for Mothers of the Church.

Church Administrator

VII.Question- What are the duties of the Church
Administrator?

A. Each local church determines the duties of the church
administrator. The scope of responsibilities and
authority varies significantly with each local
congregation, based on the needs of that
congregation. On the Downloads page of this section,
there is a link to the document "Church
Administrator Roles & Responsibilities," which goes
over what a church business administrator is and
provides a detailed accounting of what can be
included under his/her scope of responsibilities: This
resource is developed by the National Association of
Church Business Administration
https://www.nasbaregistry.org/exhibitors/national-
association-of-church-business-administration

Minister of Music/Choir President/Coordinator

VIII.Question- Does the Convention have salary
guidelines for musicians?

A. The Convention does not maintain any standards on
salaries—that is a matter completely up to the local
church and job market for musicians. However, there
is some good information available on the web. Here
are some online resources for you to explore: Bureau
of Labor Statistics:
http://www.bls.gov/ooh/entertainment-and-
sports/musicians-and-singers.htm

IX. Question- What are the duties of the Choir President or Coordinator?

A. Choir Coordinator (or President) Responsible to the Minister of Music or the Director of their particular choir • Appointed or elected • Must have a proven record of personal integrity and self-motivation in the fulfillment of the Ministry • Must be saved, talented, and Holy Spirit-filled with a desire to bring glory to God through music. • Must have a growing theology and practice of Christ-centered worship. • Must have administrative skills. Requirements: • Sufficient health to discharge duties properly • Requires passing criminal and civil background checks (particularly if working with children and youth) • Strong commitment to biblical Christian principles and teachings both professionally and personally • Must be living a Christian life in the world, and participating in Christian Bible study, particularly as provided by this church Duties: • Leads the choir leadership (administrative) staff (secretaries, treasurer, etc.) • (Unless elected) appoint (with MM and CD approval) key persons to assist, knowing that the director is ultimately responsible for the work of this choir in carrying out the administrative needs of the choir. • Enforce guidelines for choir with the approval from the choir director (uniform, conduct decorum, attendance, etc.) • Handle (or appoint someone to handle) dues, uniform fees, music fees, etc. • Track attendance, sick or missing members (see section leaders) • Seek ways to recruit new members • Keep choir morale lifted through fellowship events, visitation, cards, etc. • Comply with all administrative duties appropriate for a church staff member, i.e.

attend staff meetings, orientation training and workshops, turn in reports, stay in regular contact with the choir director • Encourage members to participate in Mass Choir opportunities for special events, i.e. Women's Day, Men's Day, Pastor and Church Anniversary, Family and Friends' Day, Easter, Christmas, etc. • Work in cooperation and Christian fellowship with other ministry staff persons.

Baptist Training Union (BTU)

X. Question- What is the BTU?

A. Baptist Training Union. Baptist Training Union has been a part of the African American Baptist Church since its early beginnings. It was a part of Christian education designed to instruct all church members in basic bible beliefs, Baptist doctrine, church membership, discipline, policy, and procedures. It was traditionally held in most Baptist Churches on Sunday evenings, prior to evening worship. It began as a training ground for young people. Consequently, the predecessor of the Baptist Training Union was the Baptist Young People's Union (BYPU). In June of 1984, President Theodore Judson Jemison of the National Baptist Convention, USA, discontinued the Baptist Training Union Board, giving its responsibilities to the Sunday School Publishing Board. As a result of this move, the SSPB formed the "Nurture for Baptist Churches (NBC). It is interesting to note that in 2003, the SSPB decided that NBC had not worked and is now in the process of re-constituting the BTU. For more information and resources about BTU, visit the Sunday School Publishing Board.

Young Matrons

XI. Question- Can someone with a minister's license obtain from the Internet pastor a Baptist Church?

A. Here are a few online resources that may help you in designing a curriculum for Young Matrons: an online resource especially for women in ministry (website, blog, Email Newsletter, support groups, etc.) sponsored by:

1. ChristianityToday.com. You may visit their website at this address: http://www.giftedforleadership.com
2. Women's Ministry Network: http://www.womensministry.net/
3. American Baptist Churches website: http://www.abc-usa.org
4. American Baptist Women In Ministry: http://www.abwim.org
5. Christianity Today: http://www.christianitytoday.com
6. RH Boyd Publishing: http://www.rhboydpublishing.com/index.php
7. Judson Press: http://www.judsonpress.com

Christian Education

XII. Question- How can the NBC accredit my church school?

A. A church can certify a school to be held at the church through the Sunday School Publishing Board (SSPB). Visit **www.sspbnbc.com** for more information.

Ministries and Missions

XIII.Question- What is the difference between a ministry and an auxiliary?

A. There isn't a standard definition, so the terms may be used interchangeably. At the National Baptist Convention, an Auxiliary is a function (department) within the organizational structure that is named in our Constitution and By-laws. Ministries within the Convention are not mentioned specifically in the Constitution and, consequently, may be more fluidly organized based on the current needs of the Convention and its constituency. In the purest sense, all auxiliaries are ministries. In the structural work of the church, they may vary slightly. An auxiliary is usually an "in-house" service agency organized to carry out perpetual Church functions, such as the choir or ushers. They are also usually responsible for raising their budget and contributing to the overall church budget. A ministry may focus more on outreach and purpose-fulfilling functions. These foundational functions will usually be funded by the church, even if they're unable to raise their budget. Again, the two terms are not mutually exclusive. For example, the choir may be an auxiliary of the church, but they are also responsible for the music ministry.

New Member Ministry

XIV.Question- Where can I find resources for new member ministries?

A. A few good resources to consider include:

1. "New Member Training" by Reverend Charles Powell
2. Huntley's Manual for Every Baptist" by Thomas Elliott Huntley. The National Baptist Sunday School Publishing Board publishes both books.
3. "A New Baptist Church Manual" published by Judson Press.

New Mission Society

XV. Question- Where can I find information about how to form a new missionary society?

A. The Foreign Mission Board of the National Baptist Convention, USA, Inc. has published a book entitled "The Missionary Workers Manual," which details the philosophy, structure, and scope of mission work. Our own Sunday School Publishing Board published it. This book is quite comprehensive and will be a great help to any Church seeking help organizing and structuring a mission program.

Foreign Missionary

XVI. Question How do I become a foreign missionary in the Baptist Church?

A. In order to become a Missionary, under the Foreign Mission Board, NBC, USA, Inc., the criteria are as follows:

1. Complete Application, with references [one must be from your Pastor] and resume`.
2. Complete at least two interviews with Executive Committee members.

3. If accepted, complete a Psychological Assessment [at the expense of the Foreign Mission Board] and a statement of physical condition from your personal physician.
4. General Orientation: Assignment will be given with a start date
5. Contract will be signed.
6. Special Orientation: Geared specifically toward the country to be assigned.

The applicant must:

a. Provide a Statement of Faith indicating your acceptance of Jesus Christ as Lord and Savior.
b. Have earned at least a bachelor's degree
c. Make a three-year commitment as a long-term missionary. The time commitment will vary for short-term missionaries [depending upon need]
d. Be willing to participate in the aforementioned application process
e. Be willing to travel to foreign mission fields {of the FMB's choosing}

Contact the Foreign Mission Board for more information: 866.494.7140

Membership

Legal Issues

XVII. Question- What guidance can you provide on how to handle registered sex offenders in the church?

A. There are good resources for you to check out on the website of Church Mutual Insurance Company. There are about 5 or 6 documents concerning Sexual Abuse and Background checks on these pages of their website:

Sex Offenders:
https://www.churchmutual.com/169/Child-and-Youth-Sexual-Abuse

Background Checks:
https://www.churchmutual.com/167/Background-Screening

Watch Care

XVIII. Question- What is "Watch Care?" Can I be an active member in a church on a temporary basis while maintaining membership in my home church?

A. Individuals may hold membership in one church at a time. "Watch Care" is a service a church provides to watch over individuals who are temporarily unable to attend the church where they hold membership. Typically, people under watch care are college students or people with jobs or other circumstances that require them to travel to other locations for an extended period of time. The person under watch care maintains their official membership with their home church while being welcomed to participate in the worship services and ministries of a local church on a temporary basis. Since they are not "official" members of the church receiving them under watch care, they generally can participate in activities and services but not hold office or participate in church voting.

Letter of Membership

XIX. Question- What is the content that goes into a Letter of Membership when a person is moving their membership from one Baptist Church to another by letter?

A. An example of such a letter might read:

Miss, Mrs., Or Mr. FULL NAME OF THE PERSON has informed us of a decision to join your church. We are delighted to recommend THE PERSON to you from the NAME OF FORMER CHURCH AND ADDRESS. THE PERSON has left in good and regular standing and was a valuable member of our church. I trust and pray SHE, OR HE will add to your ministry as SHE, OR HE did ours through the utilization of his or her giftings of the Holy Spirit. Please let us know when THE PERSON has officially become a member of your church so we can adjust our official membership directory.

The blessings of Jesus Christ upon you.

Respectfully,

_____

Chairman of the Deacon Board

_____

Membership Clerk

_____

Pastor _____

Date_____

XX. Question- What should a church receiving a letter of membership do?

A. The following steps should be followed:

1. The Pastor will have the Chairman of the Deacon Board or the Church's Membership Clerk send a letter to the former church indicating receipt of the letter of transfer.
2. The Pastor will have the letter from the former church read at the Deacon Board meeting.
3. If the former church has had a problem with the member requesting membership in the new church, the church may or may not share the nature of the problem with the new church. This usually does not happen even if there is a problem with the member.
4. The Deacon Board will vote on accepting the new member and share the name during the regular service or at a church business meeting. In some instances, the name of the person requesting membership, upon approval by the Deacon Board, will be present the name on a Sunday (usually Communion Sunday) with a motion for acceptance as a member of the new congregation. The congregation then votes for approval of the membership.
5. Either on the last Sunday or the first Sunday of the month, the newly approved members will be asked to come forward and receive a right hand of fellowship from a select group of officers on behalf of the church or the entire church with the Pastor leading the way.

Gender & Sexual Orientation

XXI.Question- Does NBC have a position on homosexual practices and the ordination of homosexual clergy?

A. The National Baptist Convention USA Inc. does not have an "official" position on any issues with regard to homosexuality. Historically, we, as a Convention, have not sought to endorse particular positions on behalf of local Baptist Churches. This is in keeping with the nature of a Baptist polity, which does not permit us to make authoritative, pontifical, doctrinal statements or creeds on behalf of our constituency. We believe in the local freedom of each member of our Convention to decide for itself on such issues as homosexuality. However, if you were to take a poll of traditional, missionary Black Baptist Churches, it is very safe to say that you will find a majority of them:

1. Against homosexuality/lesbianism as a legitimate expression of God's will.
2. Against ordaining practicing homosexuals/lesbians for any type of ministry in the Body of Christ.
3. Against, but permits persons guilty of illicit acts of a heterosexual nature, for example, adultery and fornication, to continue in the practice of ministry in the Body of Christ (with the proper accountability measures, i.e., censure, repentance, counseling, etc. in place).

XXII.Question- Does the Convention have a policy on Same-Sex Marriage?

A. The National Baptist Convention, USA, Incorporated does not dictate to its constituent churches what position to take on issues because we believe in the autonomy of the local church. However, the National Baptist Convention, USA, Inc. affirms that marriage is a sacred biblical covenant between a man and a woman.

Baptist Doctrine, Denomination, & Ordinances

Church Covenant

XXIII. Question- Which Church Covenant does the National Baptist Convention recommend?

A. The Convention doesn't have any specific policy or information on the Church Covenant. However, we have this response from a member of the Board: "The National Baptist Convention USA Inc. does not adopt church covenants. Then New Hampshire Covenant is the one most Baptist Churches use." Many churches have taken the liberty of revising/updating the church covenant to add more contemporary language and references. The New Hiscox Guide for Baptist Churches (Goodwin) has a section on the Church covenant that you may find helpful. Here's a good resource (with many more links) on Wikipedia that goes into detailed discussions of the origin of the church covenant and the different versions: http://en.wikipedia.org/wiki/New_Covenant_Theology You may also want to Google "New Hampshire Covenant" and/or search for information at the Southern Baptist Convention and the American Baptist Churches websites.

Missionary Baptist

XXIV. Question- What is the difference between a Missionary Baptist Church and a Baptist Church?

A. Most Baptist Churches are, by nature, Missionary Baptist Churches. This means that they believe in the mission work of the Church as it relates to spreading the Gospel both at home and abroad. However, there are some of the Baptist persuasion that are not "missionary," most notable among them is the Primitive Baptist Church. Historically and culturally speaking, the African American Baptist Church grew in response to the withdrawal of most white Baptist Churches (Southern Baptist Convention) from doing mission work on the continent of Africa following the Civil War. Hence, our churches were distinguished from theirs, not by terms such as "colored" or "African," as was the case with the Methodist Church, but were designated as "missionary."

Baptist/ Black Baptist

XXV. Question- What makes a Baptist a Baptist? What makes the Black Baptists different from the Southern Baptists?

A. PART 1: We are Baptist because:

1. We believe in total immersion in water based on personal confession of faith in Jesus Christ as the only source of salvation on the part of a believer.
2. We believe the most doctrinally correct church organizational decision-making structure is Congregationally Based. This means that, ultimately,

church decisions reside with the active membership on the basis of democratic voting procedures. The general example used to highlight this reality has to do with employing a pastor. Each local church interviews and offers a preacher to become its pastor. In many non-Baptist denominations, i.e., Methodists, Episcopalians, Catholics, etc., a Bishop appoints pastors to churches.

3. We believe a Christian's conscience is ultimately accountable to Christ alone, and therefore, no decisions made by others can be forced upon him or her. For example, when it comes to tithing, a person cannot be denied membership in a Baptist church because he/she doesn't believe in tithing.

4. We believe in the separation of Church and State. This simply means that the church will never be controlled by, financed by, or controlled by the city, state, or federal government.

5. We believe that each Baptist church is structurally and doctrinally independent from other Baptist Churches. We are separate and unequal. No Baptist church can be told by another Baptist church what to believe, how to think, or how to organize itself. Each is autonomous.

PART 2: Black Baptists differ from Southern Baptists: Black Baptists differ from Southern Baptists, most of all in our theological understanding of church/community relationships. We believe the church should promote justice and peacemaking legislation and policies that deal with the physical, emotional, mental, spiritual, social, political, and economic needs of not only individuals and families but, just as important, one's race. Since Blacks in America have always dealt with "racism," our understanding of the church's mission is deeply determined by our sociological status in America and the world at any given time.

Articles of Faith

XXVI.Question- Are there 18 or 24 Baptist Articles of Faith?

A. Here is a brief theological, historical, and doctrinal explanation of why some sources cite 18 and others cite 24 Baptist Articles of Faith: Firstly, we recognize the 18 Articles of Faith as listed on the National Baptist Convention website (Although The Sunday School Publishing Board sells the Busy Pastor's Guide, this does not mean that the Convention subscribes to every point of view of every author). The National Baptist Convention's history is connected to the history of all Baptist Churches in America. To make a long story (or lesson) short, the development of our denomination ought to be looked at in relation to our response to slavery and both the Southern and Northern Baptist Conventions. The Baptist Church in America adopted two statements of Faith: The Philadelphia Confession of 1742 and the New Hampshire Declaration. The Philadelphia Confession was highly Calvinistic and contained 24 Articles. The New Hampshire Declaration was revised in 1853, combining some articles and adding Articles VIII and X. It is the "declaration" upon which the National Baptist Convention was organized and contained 18 Articles.

Excommunication

XXVII.Question- By what means can a church excommunicate a member?

A. Technically, Baptists do not excommunicate. We do, however, have the right (or responsibility) to dismiss members. Baptist doctrine provides two ways of dismissal.

1. The first is by "Letter." This is when a member transfers their membership and asks for a letter.
2. The second is by "Expulsion" or "Exclusion." This may be done when any member refuses to adhere to the Bible, Baptist Doctrine, or the Rules and Regulations of that particular Church.

In all cases, the disciplinary prescription laid out in Matthew Chapter 18 must be followed.

Baptism

XXVIII.Question- Can people who are not ordained ministers conduct the ordinance of baptism?

A. "Only Ordained Deacons or Licensed Ministers under the authority of an Ordained Pastor/Minister may conduct the ordinance of Baptism. If the Ordained Pastor/Minister is present and leading the baptismal service (actually says the words), the physical immersion may be done by anyone. In fact, Jesus Himself never baptized anyone. He let His disciples do it for Him."

Chapter 6: The Association

I would not dare close this book without saying something about the Baptist association.

> XIX.   Question- What is an association? And what is the Baptist Association?
>
> A.   An association is an organization of persons or groups of persons having common interests, purposes, and or goals. The *Baptist* Association- is a self-governing fellowship of autonomous churches sharing "the common faith," Baptist Beliefs, active in Evangelism and Mission, Christian Education, and Ministry.

The Association Principle

Although Churches are distinct in respect to each particular congregation, they are one in purpose and goal, having **JESUS CHRIST** as head and Lord.   Therefore, the Associational Principle is that of interrelatedness or interdependence.   This expression of interrelatedness is best known by participation in "The Association."

During the early years of the Associational work, it was called the General Assembly.   The annual meeting was called the General Meeting.   It began as an effort to solidify established doctrinal principles and practices to eliminate the isolation of churches and to express Mutual Concern, Unified Purpose, and Kindred Fellowship in the Mission and Ministry of the Church.

The Association, as we know it, is a group of churches working to produce a perfect union to provide a more efficient means of promoting <u>Christian Education</u>, Mission Work, and

Evangelism, not only within each local congregation but throughout the world.

The Purpose of the Association

The Association may meet monthly, quarterly, and or annually, with each participating church sending representatives or delegates to the meetings. The Associational Meeting provides leadership training for local church leaders. It allows members to share and gain information and experiences that help to build the work of each local church and the Association.

The Association does not have rulership over the churches; however, at the request of any church or group thereof, it may provide leadership to settle disputes and enable Pastors to be better leaders and overseers of the flock of God. Also, each auxiliary of the Church has a similar membership within the Association.

Although it is not dictatorial, the authority of the Association and its leadership should be recognized and respected by Pastors and members of participating churches.

Pastors and Non-Pastoring Preachers need to recognize that the association is an entry into great fellowship with other ministers and churches like no other. The association seeks to train ministers to be qualified for service before being ordained and, or put to work in leadership positions. It provides not only for the teaching and the training of ministers but also others for mission work, Evangelism, and Christian Education. Finally, the association seeks to dispel false doctrinal practices and teachings and to help those churches in distress by settling grievances and disputes through Christian Education of members, as well as Ministers.

Unity Among Associations

Local Churches join forces to build an Association. Associations join forces to form the Conventions. As we contend for the Faith once delivered, we seek to provide motivation, participation, organization, budget, structure, goals, and activities, all pointing to enabling churches, associations, and the convention to be greater mission workers for the Master.

Members support the church. Churches support the Convention. Conventions support the work. What kind of supporters are we? What type of work can go forth with our support? What encouragement can be given by our practices?

In summary, the Association is a river of resources and, at the same time, the raft that reaches across the river, allowing communication and cooperation. Associational involvement is the channel between the local church and its mission and ministry to contend for the faith and inform the world that Jesus loves us and died for our sins, providing us the opportunity to help others who otherwise will be drowned by false doctrinal teachings and practices and idle negligence toward the assignment of stewardship in mission, ministry, Christian education and great fellowship to the glory of the Father.

Conclusion

Realizing that churches are autonomous, this book is designed to arouse our thinking about the issues in our Church life. This book should teach us how to answer questions that are being asked in many of today's congregations.

My prayer is that you both enjoy this book and find it to be helpful in your daily life. As seen by many of the answers provided, some issues are both avoidable and preventable.

Thank you for reading my book, and God bless you.

Dr. O. D. Woods

www.ingramcontent.com/pod-product-compliance
Lightning Source LLC
Chambersburg PA
CBHW051557120626
46551CB00013B/1555